Bring Your Crayons to the Office

A Way Forward for Playful Business Analysts and Project Managers

10 imaginative ways to facilitate persona development, user stories, team collaboration and more

CANDACE SPEARS

DEDICATION

For my hubby and my girls. You're key to my push
and drive to take knowledge and share it. Girls,
speaking out is a gift to never take for granted.
Someone needs what you have to say.

CONTENTS

INTRODUCTION: **Let's Play**

What is business analysis as compared to project management? While the methods and suggestions in this book are applicable to both skill sets, business analysis and business analysts are the primary focus here.

It can be said that project managers are responsible for delivering the solution to a problem, while business analysts are responsible for discovering the problem and determining the solution.

Traditionally, business analysts are taught to do requirements gathering and analysis, or any type of elicitation, they do so through time-consuming question and answer sessions. Such as:

"What's the first thing you do after a customer order comes in?"
"What happens after that step?"
"Who's involved at that point?"

While this line of questioning is useful and effective one-on-one, or in small groups, it becomes less effective the more people come into the mix and if the project's complexity intensifies.

It is also wanting because it can be boring. Let's face it, hours upon hours of being interviewed is less than enthralling. When boredom is at play, you can be assured that people are not as engaged as they should be and therefore may not be providing maximum value to the project.

So how do you get to the heart of understanding business needs? Say you need to uncover new processes in a way that respects project size and complexity. Still you want to keep your team engaged so that their full attention and awesome knowledge are engaged when you need them most. How can you do it?

Enter the methods found in this book: By removing the formality and replacing it with tangible, sometimes called childlike, playful activities that stimulate people to talk to each other instead of being talked to.

The activities here impel people to engage more than just their minds; they engage their bodies as they move around the room. Tactile engagement comes into play as they may shift papers and posters around. Meanwhile, thinking in pictures may free them from mental constraints or even emotional inhibitions or biases. This is a new twist for an age-old practice, and it considers all the mental, physical, and emotional parts of a team.

The International Institute of Business Analysis says:
Business analysis is used to identify and articulate the need for change in how organizations work, and to facilitate that change. As business analysts, we identify and define the

solutions that will maximize the value delivered by an organization to its stakeholders.

Business analysts work across all levels of an organization and may be involved in everything from defining strategy, to creating the enterprise architecture, to taking a leadership role by defining the goals and requirements for programs and projects or supporting continuous improvement in its technology and processes.

Okay, enough talk. Let's play.

Your next project is around the corner. The excitement of jumping onto something new, coupled with the release of delivering on the current project, is a time of both satisfaction and uncertainty.

These are some of the thoughts I have heard expressed during my career:

- "I'm happy for this project to be over; it's been a long time coming."

- "Who's involved with this new project?"

- "Is this the right thing to do instead of project B?"

- "It's about time we started focusing on this."

- "It'll be interesting to see how this turns out."

- "What's the business case?" *

These are all comments I've heard and used myself at one point or another over the course of my career. Let me tell you about me and my experience leading and guiding projects forward.

I'll be using some industry terms and catchwords that I will set off with asterisks and define in the accompanying glossary.

I have worked across many industries as a project manager and a business analyst for fields such as healthcare, manufacturing, and insurance. I've served both in marketing, product management/development, and information technology. Having experienced both waterfall and agile project methodologies, I've spent most of the time working with teams in the agile* space. Working as a project manager, product manager, and business analyst in the traditional sense, on the agile side of things I've been a coach, a scrum master* and product owner* for various agile teams.

Inspiring others to engage, sharing common goals, and being expressive amid these ideals, these activities keep a project moving in the right direction with clarity and value at the helm so that the project moves forward as the team delivers business value as its highest priority.

I'm presenting 10 methods I've used to facilitate this engagement across my time in various industries. The methods can be employed regardless of industry, company type or size. Exploring these methods is timely for you if you're facing the next project, or are in the middle of one that's already underway but you haven't gathered the key pieces of information that take the team and delivery to the next level.

We'll explore everything from developing personas*to understanding how to leverage emotions and gauge the temperature of a team. We'll delve into how to pull out user stories*. And we'll even approach future business processes. These methods are simple, step-by-step, and practical approaches to tackling a specific information need while keeping the team highly engaged.

From having worked in marketing and the information technology space, I know these worlds engage different mindsets. One tends to favor creativity and right brain activity over the more analytical, left brain work. For project managers and business analysts, when these two worlds collide, you get the mix of creativity and logical thought you will read in this book.

But beware, this mix is not always welcomed with open arms since people tend to lean one way or the other. In the last chapter, you'll understand more about the challenges that come with employing this skill set mix.

If you're ready to kick into gear and employ tested approaches that will move the needle, then this book is for you. Simply grab your crayons, turn the page and get to work.

CHAPTER 1

Who is your audience?

The stage is set and the actors are in place. As the curtain rises, the cast, dressed in startling clown costumes, fill the stage and begin to growl like tigers. At that moment, a sea of cries is heard from the audience. Those shrieks are coming from terrified toddlers whose parents thought they

1

were taking them to see Cuddly and the friendly clowns. Instead, they got Clarence and his insane troupe of Bozos. Shiver.

This brief scene is one you want to avoid: you're set to embark on a project and bring people together but you may fail to understand the audience – and all the while your audience may fail to understand their purpose in coming together. Like our unlucky audience above, this can be a nightmare.

Before undergoing any type of collaborative process, stop and understand what the goals might be. Know what unique perspectives your attendees may bring to this project. Ask yourself these three questions when preparing for a session:

1. Why do the attendees think they are coming to this session? If you've spelled this out clearly in your pre-meeting communications, this should be straightforward. Have you done so?

2. What motivates them to attend? Do they have a vested interest in the topic? Were they "voluntold" to attend and act as a representative? Will the outcome affect their job responsibilities or income?

3. What do you know about their characters or personalities? This may not be easy to determine if you're brought into to a session of people you haven't worked with before. Motivating people to collaborate and express ideas is part

science but in large part, psychology. It requires a lot of creativity.

What do you understand about them? For example, lighthearted Sally loves to make jokes at every interaction. Jalen, however, tends to be quiet in meetings, but he can clearly put together a snapshot of a problem and potential solutions. Knowing your people will help you facilitate a session that taps into the attendees' characters and strengths, keeping them open and engaged.

When you know the characters of the attendees, you can leverage them. For instance, how might we take advantage of what we know about Sally and Jalen?

Let's say your first session involves working in teams. If someone in the group, we'll call him Will, tends to be on the quieter side and less willing to speak up in meetings, then pairing him with Sally is a great idea. Engage her strength in social situations to bring out Will's voice.

On the other hand, someone like Jalen is good at summarizing problems and solutions. It's likely he will pair well with a team that includes creative, big idea thinkers whom he can keep grounded.

While it is important to think about the goal when bringing people together, it's even more important that the participants share the process of setting goals. When everyone shares in crafting the goal, the skin is in the game, so to speak, and participants are committed.

The quickest way to cut off expression from participants is to prescribe a goal. You're probably thinking that this sounds like a contradiction. You may be asking yourself: "How do I align people with a goal before the meeting starts, yet set a goal during the meeting?"

Let's consider for a moment the distinction between goals and objectives in this context. Let's call putting people together to create a next-step action plan an *objective.* People are coming together to be informed of a mission.

Whereas, understanding and acting on the mission is the *goal* that the team should uncover. It can happen once you're together or it can happen prior to the meeting with a subset of people. Either way, you want to make sure sufficient skin, that is commitment, is in the game. We will explore more about this later.

Now that we've nailed down the audience, let's keep rolling.

CHAPTER 2

Persona Development

As we noted in the glossary, a persona is "the aspect of someone's character that is presented to or perceived by others."

In business, these are the people or roles you serve in some capacity. For example, let's say we are building an American Girl doll, one key persona might be a 10-12-year-old girl. Another key persona may be a parent, perhaps a woman, age 35-50 with an income range of $95,000 -

8

$200,000 who would be likely to buy such a toy for her daughter. In other words, understanding a persona requires a grasp of the demographics and psychographics of your industry's users and influencers.

This is essential: By understanding the perspective and surrounding detail of the people we are targeting with our product or message, we get closer to making sure we are building the appropriate product or service for them.

Everyone who observes these personas will see them differently, depending on their unique points of view. Organizing and engaging teams are the best ways to eliminate the bias towards what we know or think we know. Here are two methods to use for creatively developing personas:

Method 1: A picture is worth a thousand words

Materials needed: Crayons, colored pencils, or markers, poster -sized sheets of paper.

Note on team size and assembly: Break into teams of two to three depending on your group or do this as an individual exercise if everyone is knowledgeable enough.

Just as it's important to understand everyone's personalities and characters, it's important to understand everyone's knowledge level ahead of time; or you can create a mix of the individuals in the teams to even out the knowledge level.

Directions:

1. Kick off by asking the team to shout out a list of people who will have "interaction" with the product.

2. After creating this list, divide the teams and allow each to choose a persona or two to work on.

2. After the choices are made, allot each team 15 minutes to describe in pictures this persona/role and his/her needs. No text is allowed.

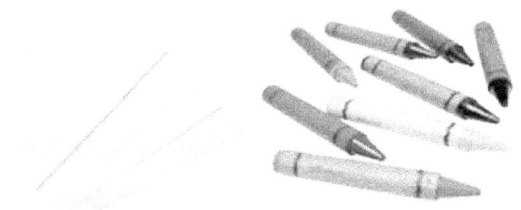

Figure 2.1: Preparing for persona drawings

Questions to consider:

Who is this person?

What does this person do?

What is their interaction with this product?

What are their needs?

What are their fears?

Remember, no text is allowed.

Method 2: Stick figures

This activity works well when you're short on time and you want to represent key personas simply as discussions continue.

Materials needed: Pre-drawn stick figures on paper and colored pens.

Directions:

1. Provide sheets of paper with stick figures pre-drawn.

2. Instruct participants to name only the roles that will interact with the product.

3. Once complete, open dialogue about who has been identified and determine what will be your agreed upon personas moving forward.

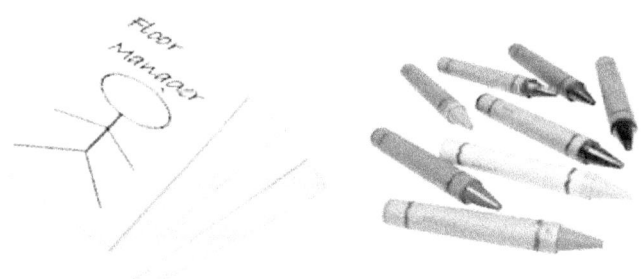

Figure 2.2: Preparing to identify personas by role

You can run this as an activity that each participant does individually. Then have everyone compare the results to ensure there are no gaps. Or if we are speaking of a team, they can name them off, using a scribe to add the title to each stick figure on the paper.

In this exercise, although you are not going into depth exploring the surrounding demographics and psychographics of the persona in question, you are providing a visual reminder to the team to consider specific roles as they execute further project discussions and plans.

You may want to explore these roles more thoroughly at some point if you have the full team engaged. But in a pinch, and to ease an unfamiliar project team in to the concept of creating personas, this is a good start.

CHAPTER 3

Identifying a Future Process or Solution

Often, when you approach work iteratively, building a vision for the future is critical to ensuring that you're keeping the full picture in mind. It's also important to help you go faster. For example, if choosing to build a new enterprise data repository, devote some high-level thought to what key subject areas may exist and their relationship. This view could affect naming conventions and table design and ensure scalability. In this example, you see how understanding a vision for the future lays the ground for just enough infrastructure and architecture to get started. Still, it allows for expanded features and value without wasted work and minimal re-work.

That said, the key is "just enough." When exploring a vision for the future, keep in mind that acting on the entire vision in one swoop can set you up for a long, inefficient waterfall* approach. Instead, do just enough to inform you of your goal and make smart decisions. For your first release, leave the nitty gritty detail only to that segment you plan to focus on. Chapter three on user stories* gets you to the right level of detail for your focused segment.

In a future business process, two fun methods can be used together or alone. Let's explore.

Method 1: Story mapping

Materials needed: Flip chart paper, sticky notes, and blank sheets of paper.

Directions:

1. Identify your primary goal. This can be the overall project goal, the end goal of a process or some other defined goal inherent to the project.

2. To identify the "primary goal," ask the question, "What will be achieved when this business process is complete?"

3. Using this goal, agree on and lay out the user flow to get there. What high-level

steps must happen to reach the goal?

4. Have the team identify features at every flow step: You can separate the group into teams by flow steps, or if you have a mix of people from different business areas, let each small group identify features for the entire flow.

Know that while story mapping can be applied to a narrow and focused goal, you can also use it to approach a broader business process.

Primary Goal: Make a donation

Figure 3.1: Step 1 – Identify primary goal

Primary Goal: Make a donation

User Flow in Reaching Goal

| Select Charity | Determine Amount | Keep Record |

Figure 3.1: Step 2 – Flow of user activity

Figure 3.3: Step 3 – Adding features

Method 2: Compare and Contrast

This is an approach I created to envision the future playfully and creatively. It also serves to take a step back and evaluate what has changed.

Materials needed: Flip chart paper, colored markers, crayons, and/or colored pencils. Work can proceed in teams or individually.

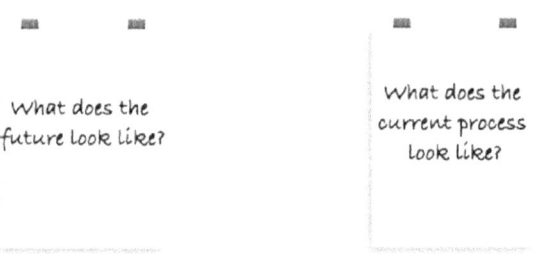

Figure 3.4: Compare and contrast

Directions:

1. To Team 1, pose the question, "What does the future look like?" The participants can express the future in pictures, connecting the story together in a process fashion.

Have yourself or a co-facilitator take notes as the teams present their process. It's helpful to have an observer when drawings are involved so that there is additional context to pass along after the activity.

To Team 2, have them illustrate the current process.

2. After the 10 or 15 minutes you've indicated, have each team post their processes to the wall. Ask Team 1, to review Team 2's work and note down

21

what has changed between the current process team two has drawn, and the future process team one has drawn.

3. For Team 2, provide them dots or mini page stickies and instruct them to place the sticky on the future process (Team 1's work) wherever they have a question or concern.

4. After these two activities are complete, direct the teams to reassemble. Team 1 should then explain the future process and allow those who placed stickies to voice their thoughts. Then, Team 1 can talk through what they saw as different and what stayed the same. Take note of any relevant discussion and factor it into your new process.

CHAPTER 4

Creating User Stories* or Requirements*

It seems obvious but it must be said that figuring out what work needs to be done is essential to doing the work. That no one would argue. The word for that process has traditionally been called requirements gathering*. Those working in agile* know this set of line by line demands or requirements as user stories*. No matter what

23

camp or terminology you're familiar with, the goal is to understand "the what." What do we need to deliver this project?

The user story offers more background than the requirement since it provides a narrative that illuminates what is guiding the client's request. Often, it also provides more flexibility to the technical team in determining how to get the project done.

Your user story generally takes a format of "As a_____ I want to_____so that I can_____. And it looks for the attached acceptance criteria, that is: "What must be present for the story to be deemed acceptable by the requestor?"

Take the example below of a user story for a non-profit donation system:

As a donor, I want to receive a receipt so that I can file it for my taxes.

In contrast, requirements written for this same body of work would look like this...

Provide a receipt

Now, that we recognize the difference between a user story and the requirement, we can feel grounded enough to talk about ways to derive user stories. In this process, we're going to pick up from story mapping* we talked about in chapter 3.

Once you have defined the primary goal and the supporting user requirements, each of the features or key items represents a potential user story. In some cases, the items may become acceptance

25

criteria on another story; but you'll have to sort through the whole project's details to determine this. As a team, here are two ways to approach this task:

Method 1: Pick a feature and bring the team

Materials needed: Features from story mapping on sticky notes, markers and poster sized sheets of paper or a whiteboard.

Directions:

1. Pick out feature items from the story map, divide them among the business team to create the stories. A mix of business and technical teams is most appropriate, assuming you have multiple representatives from the business side.

2. Allow an appropriate time limit, corresponding with the number of

features, to let the team(s) create the user
stories

Be aware that here may not a be a one for one
correlation between a user story and a feature. A
feature may end up being a piece of acceptance
criteria in a story, and you could have two or
more features roll into a single story.

Method 2: 1X1 and lead by example
Materials needed: None

Directions:

1. If you have a business analyst, or a
    product owner, the main business lead for
    the project, you can work with them one
    on one. Lead with an example story, then
    continue creating a backlog of user stories
    based off the items identified from the

story map. However, you will have to explain and present these stories to the delivery team eventually, so it's nice to have the technical team in on the ground floor as in method 1. Do what is best, given your project's constraints.

In both activities, ask the team to complete the sentence...

As a "Insert name of the actor or persona"

I want to "What is to be accomplished. What does the feature say?"

So that I can "Why does this need to be accomplished?"

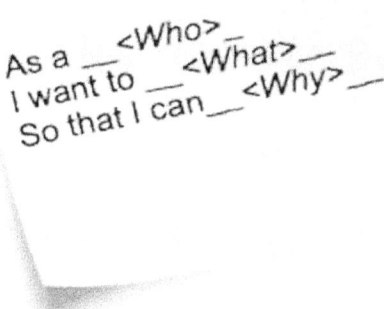

Figure 4.1; User Story format

The next piece is the acceptance criteria.

List the items that must be present for the story to be deemed acceptable.

In our donation system example, the acceptance criteria may look like this.

User story:

> *As a donor, I want to receive a receipt so that I can file it for my taxes.*

Acceptance Criteria:

> *Receipt should contain amount and date of donation.*
> *Receipt should contain donor's name.*
> *Receipt should be available to print as soon as the donation is made.*
> *Receipt should contain the organization's name and tax identification code.*

When creating these stories, you may want to capture them electronically for portability and updating.

These stories can also be created using index cards. Describe the story on the front of the card and the acceptance criteria on the back. If you have space and are posting the stories for the full team to see, you can work from these cards directly.

Know that this is not a once and done activity. User stories are living and can change; more information may be added as the project continues or product lives through to its next release.

CHAPTER 5

Prioritizing Work

Priorities, priorities, priorities. You can often hear those words chanted in office buildings or among groups of people looking to accomplish something. But, sometimes, a chant can be just that – words spoken during in-flight projects and to-do lists. When you're armed with just enough information to accomplish your goal, you'll often find yourself asking, "What do I do first?"

Pay close attention to this chapter if you've done…wait for it…any of the previous exercises. At this point, especially if you've created stories or established a new business process, you know very well that there is a lot of work ahead. Now that we know what we want to accomplish, it's time to pick something and run.

Motto of prioritization: High value work first.

If that work of value is too large, find a way to make it small enough to accomplish yet still provide solid value over the alternatives.

For example, let's take the two choices below:

> *Build a new feature that allows donors to see a log of all donations made by the*

agency with an electronic paper trail, providing moderate user delight.

Or

Build a feature that proposes to donors' participating agencies in need of funds by category and location. Such a feature could increase fundraising dollars by 40% over the previous year.

Here are a couple creative approaches to figuring out what's high value and still have a team of folks or sometimes an individual be clear on what the priority should be.

Method 1: Put your money in the right place
Materials needed: Fake money. Whether it's hundreds or thousands of dollars, depending on team size, the amount is up to you.

Also, posters or papers of the priorities to choose from with relevant descriptions.

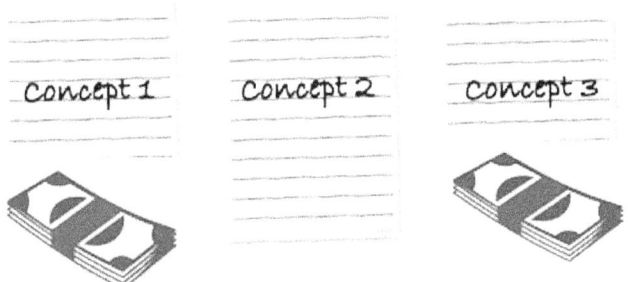

Figure 4.2: Prioritizing with money

Directions:

1. Allot each participant the same amount of cash.

2. Ask the participants where they want to spend their money. Allow them 10-15 minutes to review. Encourage the participants to talk to each other.

35

3. At the end of the time, count the cash. The priority order lies with the highest amount of cash received. After you've revealed the priority, allow for discussion around the top two or three results. Do people agree? Why or why not?

Remember, communication is important, and these exercises will allow you to get at the heart of what people are thinking when they may not have been able to express it otherwise.

Method 2: Give me a dot, or a cow

Materials needed: Dot or animal stickers, food stickers, whatever you'd like so long as they are all as the same of your choice or markers.

Also, posters or papers of the priorities with the descriptions.

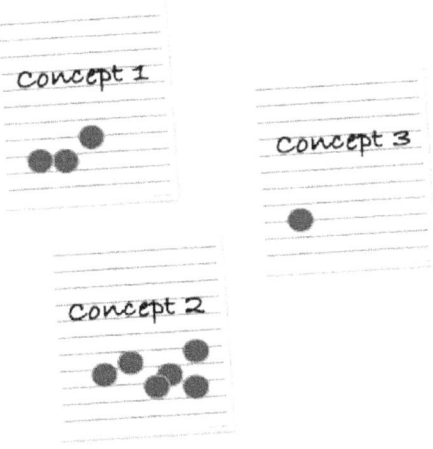

Figure 4.3: Prioritizing with stickers, markers.

Directions:

1. Like method one, make visible the priority options. This time place them on a wall and give a fair amount of space between each so there is not congestion while

people are standing and reading. Allocate the same number of stickers to each person, or tell them they can place X number of dots if using a marker.

2. Now, just as exercise one, provide a time limit, tally, and the priorities are determined.

CHAPTER 6

Gauging Emotional Temperature

It can be hard to get a true sense of a team's feelings toward a project at any given time. While it appears, we should all just roll up our sleeves and get over the emotional stuff, still getting an accurate gauge of people's insights and biases is important. The writings of organization science and applied psychology journals highlight this very thing.

"Positive emotions in the workplace help employees obtain favorable outcomes including achievement, job enrichment and higher quality social context." [1]

"Negative emotions, such as fear, anger, stress, hostility, sadness, and guilt, however increase the predictability of workplace deviance,"[2]

Emotions play a critical role and, in a collaboration, everyone has some level of contribution, responsibility and a stake in the game. What happens when people disengage or harbor negative emotions but won't share them? What happens when fear, sabotage or perhaps a passive aggressive personality trait takes hold? Let's look at an example:

Meet Brandon, he's leading a team meeting and he highlights the accomplishment of completing the design review with the architecture team. No sooner than the accomplishment is celebrated, a voice across the table shouts, "Well, why didn't we see the design? Don't underestimate our ability to understand what goes into that process."

Now Brandon, has a situation to diffuse. His intention was to highlight team members' accomplishments but it's come at the peril of others feeling excluded, which could lead to disengagement. After setting the record straight, he needs to command and openly acknowledge the team's feelings, what concerns them, what motivates them, so that the project moves forward and the team adopts a healthy working environment.

We'll explore three techniques to gauge the team's temperature, help them reflect, and correct course.

Method 1: I'm Nervous, I'm excited, I wish.

Materials needed: Three poster-sized sheets of paper, markers, sticky notes

Directions:

1. Write these three statements (one for each sheet) at the top of the paper:

    I'm nervous about...

    I'm excited about...

    I wish...

2. Ask the group to take five to seven minutes to reflect on a response to each of these statements. Have them write their response, one thought per sticky note, then post them to the appropriate board.

3. When all have posted their input, take five minutes for the team to walk and observe the responses. Ask them to group responses together where they see duplication or commonality.

4. Finally, use a marker and allocate two dots per person to place on the response(s) they feel the most strongly about. Doing this will give you a good idea where the key issues are that need attention or bright spots to tout and/or leverage as motivation.

Method 2: Emoji me

Materials needed: Three poster-sized sheets of paper, markers, sticky notes

Directions:

1. Draw a happy, sad, and neutral emoji (as indicated in the picture below). Like the previous exercise. This will represent a range of emotions, but using a picture instead of words. Imagery works well in connecting with emotion and eliciting a response.

2. Follow steps two to four indicated in activity one.

Figure 6.1: "Emoji me" team temperature gauge

The work does not stop after these exercises are complete. No, it's just beginning. The output of these exercises will have enlightened you. What you do with that insight affects the health of the team, and how you can either correct their course, or further the team down an open and transparent path. Let's look at the next steps following these two exercises.

45

• Isolate the key issues or bright spots and do something with that information. For example, if "unrealistic timelines" bubbled up as a key issue, propose to the team a roundtable or planning session around the work on their plate. They can reevaluate what dates they can commit to. If a bright spot of "Good support from the research and development team" bubbles up, make it known. Communicate it to R&D with the team's participation and continue to let what is working well continue to flourish.

[1] Staw, B.M., Sutton, R. S., Pelled, L.H. (1994). Employee positive emotion and favorable outcomes at the workplace. Organization Science, 5(1) 51-70.

[2] Lee, Kibeom, & Allen, Natalie J. (2002). Organizational Citizenship Behavior and Workplace Deviance: The Role of Affect and Cognitions. Journal of Applied Psychology, 87(1), 131-142.

CHAPTER 7

The Challenges Ahead

"Crayons and drawing, I feel like I'm in elementary school," says a critic. "This is the digital age. Why waste time putting stuff on paper?"

Expect comments like these. Childhood is often thought of as the time when we were most creative or at the least most willing to express our thoughts and ideas. We were uninhibited by the thoughts of others, simply due to our lack of experience in the world and own selfish desires. Paul Sloan of Destination-Innovation.com comments,

> *"Children have the benefit of not knowing what is not possible. For them everything is feasible."*

Adopting a childlike attitude means you open the possibility of explosive ideas and engagement with others. These are key to propelling your projects forward.

To the rebel who balks at the idea of writing anything on paper anymore, note that the use of technology alone does not make a creative and collaborative environment. True enough, we have fantastic tools today that allow us to come together and work virtually. However, there is no replacement for the tactile and social response received from drawing a picture in collaboration with another human being, or shifting sticky notes while discussing priorities.

That said, there may be times when collaborative technology is your only option. Especially, if you're utilizing remote teams. The work can still be accomplished, but you must understand that technology and tools alone aren't always a silver bullet. As mentioned in Chapter 6, there is some associated emotional psychology that taints or affects your work process. Positive emotions coupled with a push to get people out of their comfort zone helps bring brilliance to the forefront. You'll have to consider this no matter what high tech or low tech tools you utilize.

Comments from outside the team will come if you're making the team's work visible. Hang the artifacts of your sessions on walls, create a story in a hallway or room. The benefits are two-fold; One, it allows a space of ideas and context in which a team can come together and think, discuss, make decisions. Two, it provides a sense of accomplishment. Observing non-team members looking and commenting on your team's work can instill a sense of expertise and pride.   Some comments will be positive, others negative. Always take them in stride and determine if they're usable or should be ignored.

If what you do is outside of the normal, expect challenges. As part of Apple's, Think Differently campaign Steve Jobs said it best...

> *"Here's to the crazy ones — the misfits,*
> *the rebels, the troublemakers, the round*
> *pegs in the square holes. The ones who*
> *see things differently — they're not fond of*
> *rules. You can quote them, disagree with*
> *them, glorify or vilify them, but the only*
> *thing you can't do is ignore them because*
> *they change things. They push the human*
> *race forward, and while some may see*
> *them as the crazy ones, we see genius,*
> *because the ones who are crazy enough to*
> *think that they can change the world, are*
> *the ones who do."*

Crazy may become a descriptor for you, but at the
end, comments and pushback are worth it. With
the use of every tactic you should be moving the
team closer to delivering something of value.
And, in that delivery, be laser-focused about
getting to value quickly. Let me stress, a complete

project is better than a perfect approach to the project. You can go back and adjust but you need to first get to the finish line to know the right tweaks to make.

In all, grab your crayons and get to work. The people you are working with are likely in need of a shakeup to bring the life, collaboration and plain fun back into their jobs, so go deliver something awesome together.

GLOSSARY

Agile

This method of project management or project delivery divides tasks into short iterations of value-driven work and frequent reassessments.

Business analyst

This professional is responsible for uncovering business needs, mapping business processes, and bridging any communication gap between the technical team and the business.

Persona

Broadly speaking, a persona is an aspect of a character that is perceived by or presented to others. In business, a persona is an end-user or a role whom the analyst and project manager serve in some capacity by understanding that targeted person's demographic and psychographic information.

Product Owner

Taken from the Scrum methodology of Agile. This person is responsible for laying out the product or solution vision and creating the user stories that spell out the key features necessary to achieve it. This person has the authority to prioritize what user stories or features get delivered for a given release. In an agile world, a business analyst may work closely with this person to craft user stories.

Project manager

This professional is responsible for managing the project to its completion.

The project manager has authority to act on a project and in some cases secure resources when appropriate. The project manager plays a major role in communicating with all stakeholders.

Requirements gathering

This refers to the research for discovering customer's needs, and justifying or preparing for the project's development.

Scrum Master

This person is responsible for facilitating the team's meetings which may include 15-minute daily stand up meetings, planning sessions, and user story refinement. This person, a role also taken from the Scrum methodology of Agile, also has the job of removing any impediments to the team's work. This person can be a technical team member. In any many cases, the traditional business analyst role is evolving into a scrum master, assuming the tasks of both a business analyst and a project manager. However, in the Scrum methodology the project management team is self-managed.

Story mapping

This technique uses the user's perspective for generating a set of user stories. Each high-level user activity can be broken down into workflow that can be further decomposed into a set of detailed tasks.

User story

Used in the agile approach of project management for software development, this technique captures the description of a software feature from the end-user's perspective.

Waterfall

Unlike the agile method, this approach toward project management requires sequential stages and a fixed plan of work. Each phase of the waterfall project must be complete before moving on to the next.

ABOUT THE AUTHOR

Candace Spears is a technology leader, innovator, mom, and now wears the hat of an author. With over a decade of experience across business intelligence, marketing, and product development, Candace has been involved in creating data and analytic solutions, software products, and marketing campaigns for top companies including GE, Brady Corp., We Energies, and MGIC Corp.

In the corporate world, it is a lot of hard work and consumption of experiences that help either grow careers, or sink them. In Candace's case, her vast array of challenges in the workforce, as a manager, a woman, a mother, and wife; has lead her to much success. Now she looks to give back to others hoping to take the same route.

Bring Your Crayons to the Office

Her first book, "Bring Your Crayons to the Office" enlists several of her past experiences, as well as real one on one advice about how to be effective in collaborating with people to gather information, get projects completed and products brought to market.

Candace was born and raised in Milwaukee, WI but shares lessons that can be used by anyone around the globe. It is not easy to share your failures and your successes all in the same breath. However, Candace has found an even balance that works for her, and just may work for her readers.

Find out more at CandaceSpears.com

Dear readers, may I Ask a Favor?

If you enjoyed this book, found it useful or otherwise then I'd really appreciate it if you would post a short review on Amazon. I do read all the reviews personally so that I can continually write what people are wanting.

Thanks,

Candace Spears

Notes:

Notes:

Notes:

www.ingramcontent.com/pod-product-compliance
Lightning Source LLC
Chambersburg PA
CBHW071755170526
45167CB00003B/1033